THE LORD'S PRAYER

Rose Visual Bible Studies

ROSE
PUBLISHING

The Lord's Prayer
Rose Visual Bible Studies

Published by Rose Publishing
An imprint of Tyndale House Ministries
Carol Streams, Illinois
rose-publishing.com

ISBN 978-1-62862-966-8

Author: Titus O'Bryant, ThM, Teaching Pastor, Grace Fellowship Church

Printed in the United States of America
31 30 29 28 27 26 25
9 8 7 6 5 4 3

Contents

"This, then, is how you should pray..."

Matthew 6:9

The Lord's Prayer

Pine processionary caterpillars are fascinating little creatures. They trail after one another in long lines, head following tail, looking something like a very long snake.

The nineteenth-century French naturalist and botanist, Jean-Henri Fabre, took an interest in these little creatures and conducted an experiment. He placed the caterpillars onto a line he created around the rim of potted palm plant and then watched to see what would happen. As one might suspect, they formed a line and marched in an endless circle around the rim of the pot. Fabre tried to draw them away from their circle. He put pine needles (which they like to eat) on the ground, but for seven days the caterpillars still just followed one another in their endless march.

Finally, on the eighth day, one caterpillar struck off across the inside of the pot and climbed to the top of the palm plant, but then he went back down and around the edge of the pot again. A little while later, another led the group down the outside of the pot and then turned around to come back up to the rim and continue the circle. Eventually, one intrepid caterpillar made it all the way to the ground and the rest followed as they found their way back home in the pine trees.

Now what are we to learn from Fabre and his unusual experiment? (Well, besides the obvious fact that nineteenth-century French botanists are cruel and likely to perform strange experiments with caterpillars.) If there's any kind of lesson to take from the similarities between humans and caterpillars, it just might be that change is hard. Most of us find security in predictability. Even when that predictability leads to endless circles that we'd like to escape, it can still be difficult to break our harmful patterns.

Jesus came into our world bringing change. He changes everything: our relationship with God, our view of the world, our carefully constructed priorities, and our understanding of ourselves. His teachings were a radical departure from everything that came before—the way he talked about God as our Father, about forgiveness, about our relationships with one another … and about how we *pray*.

Each of the six sessions in this study will focus on one particular phrase from the Lord's Prayer in Matthew 6:9–13, combined with a passage from Jesus' experiences and teachings from the Gospels. Along with questions to guide your study, you will also find optional Bible readings that can contribute to your prayer life, as well as prayer exercises to build your relationship with God. Just as Jesus challenged his first disciples, every line in the Lord's Prayer challenges us today to set aside our predictable notions of God and our harmful habits that give us a false sense of security, and instead to turn our gaze upward in prayer to our Father in heaven.

THE LORD’S PRAYER

Our Father in heaven,
hallowed be your name,

your kingdom come,

your will be done,
on earth as it is in heaven.

Give us today our daily bread.

And forgive us our debts,
as we also have forgiven our debtors.

And lead us not into temptation,
but deliver us from the evil one.

(Matthew 6:9–13 NIV)

OUR FATHER

Our Father who art in heaven,
hallowed be thy name;
thy kingdom come.
Thy will be done
on earth, as it is in heaven.
Give us this day our daily bread,
and forgive us our trespasses,
as we forgive those who trespass against us;
and lead us not into temptation,
but deliver us from evil.
Amen.

(traditional wording)

1 OUR FATHER IN HEAVEN

Hallowed Be Your Name

Our Father in Heaven

What is prayer? How does it work? Why should we pray? Is God moved to take decisive action that alters our reality because of prayer, or as the sovereign, all-knowing Lord, doesn't he already know exactly what the future holds? These questions tug at the edges of our imagination as we talk with God in prayer and study about prayer in the Bible.

While some element of mystery will always exist around prayer, we know that God has chosen to work through prayer to change us and to change our world. There is no question that prayer establishes a relational link between us and God, and that God works through that connection to re-order and re-organize our life just as he also changes the world in which we live.

Jesus taught his followers how to pray by giving them a model prayer recorded in Matthew 6:9–13. This prayer has been called the Lord's Prayer and it is far more than mere words we repeat. It provides a pattern to follow as we form our own personal prayers to God. Think of this prayer like a photographer creating a collection of portraits by zooming in, zooming out, then zooming back in on his subject. Our model prayer begins with a singular focus on God himself; then zooms out to God's plan and work in his world; and then zooms back in to specific needs we experience and our petitions for his help.

Read It

Key Bible Passage

For this session, read the Lord's Prayer in Matthew 6:9–13.

Also read Jesus' prayer in John 17:20–26, along with his teaching in John 16:5–15.

Optional Reading

Observe how the disciples Peter and John (who were taught how to pray by Jesus) prayed when they experienced persecution in Acts 4:23–31.

"Our Father in heaven, hallowed be your name."

MATTHEW 6:9

Know It

1. Why might the Lord's Prayer begin with a request concerning God himself: "Hallowed be your name"?

2. In John 17:20–26, who is Jesus praying for and what are his specific requests?

3. From John 16:5–15, why would Jesus say that it's better for the disciples if he goes away and sends the Holy Spirit?

Explore It

Father, Son, and Holy Spirit

As Christians, we believe in one God who exists eternally in three Persons of Father, Son, and Holy Spirit. We do *not* believe in three gods, nor do we believe in one God who only manifests himself in three or more different ways. These three Persons are all equally God. One Person is not a little more or a little bit less God than the others. They are equally God. This is what we call the Trinity.

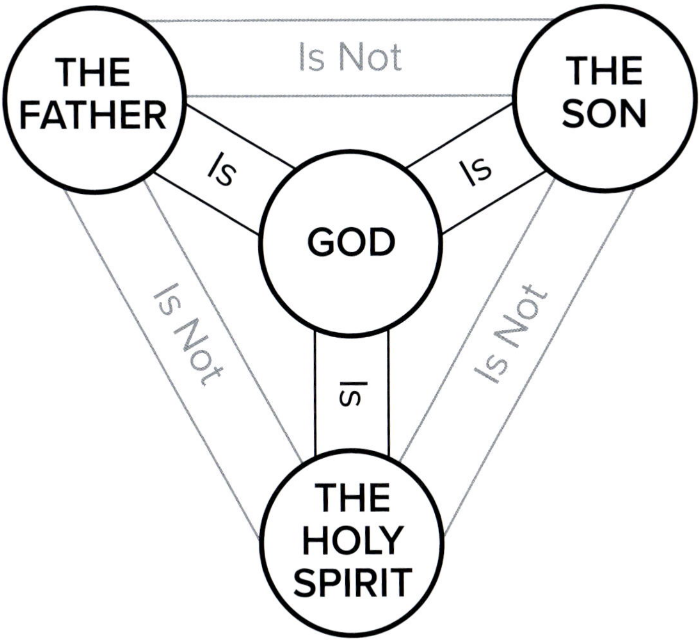

This diagram, called the shield of the Trinity, helps explain the unity and diversity of the Trinity. You can see that the Father is God, but he is not the same Person as the Son or Spirit. In the same way, the eternal Son of God (Jesus Christ) is God, but he is a different Person than the Spirit or Father. The Holy Spirit is God and is not the same Person as the Son or Father.

While each member of the Trinity is fully and equally divine, each Person also has distinct roles.

- **THE FATHER** is portrayed in the Bible as the planner and the source. He sent the eternal Son of God into our world. God the Father is the originator of all things, who was active in creation along with God the Son and God the Spirit.
- **THE SON** (Jesus Christ) existed in eternity past with the Father and the Spirit, but he took on humanity, was born into our world without ever having been made, and demonstrated to us the character of God. He revealed through his life and teaching who God is most clearly. His death and resurrection demonstrated his supremacy and make a way for us to enter into relationship with God.
- **THE HOLY SPIRIT** has been sent into our world and our lives by the Father and the Son. He is active and present in our world right now. When we trust in Jesus' finished work on the cross, the Spirit indwells us, taking up residence in our lives. He empowers us with gifts and strengths for service. He places us in the church, the body of Christ, and he guides us and leads us throughout life. He provides comfort when we grieve and strength when we are weak.

What Does It Mean to "Hallow" God's Name?

To *hallow* means to make holy. To hallow God's name means to honor it as sacred. When we pray, we enter the presence of God with reverence, worship, and thanksgiving. We thank God not only for what he has done, but also for who he is. God's greatness and glory alone are worthy of praise. In this way, we recognize that everything we have belongs to God.

While these three Persons are distinct, they exist in unity. Wherever one is present, the others are also present. They exist and work in an interpenetrating relationship. That's why Jesus could say, "If you've seen me, you've seen the Father" (from John 14:5–14). That's why we can refer to the Holy Spirit as the Spirit of Christ—because where one member of the Trinity exists all three are present.

It's also important to note that there is no fourth member in this Trinity. We are not on a journey to become gods; that is an impossibility. However, we are called into relationship with the eternal God through the Person of the Holy Spirit. We receive eternal life as a gift from God when we respond to him with faith. As we grow in our Christian life, prayer is a vital link in our relationship with God.

The Seven Petitions

The seven petitions of the Lord's Prayer emphasize various attributes of God that help us place our needs and desires in proper perspective. The first three center on God. Only by focusing on our Father in heaven can we find the attitude that puts our own needs in perspective. The next four center on our needs—body, soul, and spirit—and the needs of others.

	PETITION	THE LORD'S PRAYER	GOD'S ATTRIBUTE	MEANING
		Our Father in heaven,	God's Love	God is a loving Father.
"Your"	1	Hallowed be your name,	God's Holiness	God's name is holy.
"Your"	2	Your kingdom come,	God's Sovereignty	There is no one above God our King.
"Your"	3	Your will be done, on earth as it is in heaven.	God's Authority	God's will is perfect.
"Us/Our"	4	Give us today our daily bread.	God's Providence	Our needs are met by our heavenly Father.
"Us/Our"	5	And forgive us our debts [trespasses], as we also have forgiven our debtors [those who trespass against us].	God's Mercy	Forgiveness is our greatest need.
"Us/Our"	6	And lead us not into temptation,	God's Protection	Trials prove our faith and develop character.
"Us/Our"	7	But deliver us from the evil one.	God's Deliverance	We are more than conquerors through Christ.

Live It

Jesus taught us to pray starting with the words, "Our Father in heaven." Perhaps you've repeated those words so often that they roll from your tongue in an almost-commonplace fashion. But this way of addressing God was nothing less than revolutionary in Jesus' day.

Pagan peoples who worshiped idols and myths—such as the Romans worshiping Jupiter or the Greeks worshiping Zeus—may have sometimes referred to their god as "father." However, they used the term to indicate their god was the origin or source of all things, not to imply a family relationship with the deity.

Although Old Testament passages occasionally refer to a notion of God as Father (Deut. 14:1–2; Ps. 103:13; Jer. 31:20), Judaism by the time of Jesus considered calling God "our Father" to be presumptuous and blasphemous. Jesus, however, repeatedly called God *Father* (this was one reason the Jewish leaders wanted to execute him). When we speak to God as *our Father,* we use the intimate language of a child communicating with a loving parent.

We pray to God as our Father because that is what Jesus taught us to do and because we have been adopted as children into the family of God. We become children of God by faith in his Son, Jesus Christ (John 1:12), and so we can boldly approach God in prayer. Our Father is near to us and accessible; but he is also "in heaven," which reminds us that he is above us and greater than we are. He sees our end from the beginning and is worthy of our trust.

Life Application Questions

1. What does it mean for you to keep God's name holy—to "hallow" his name?

2. When you consider how God is our Father in heaven, what comes to mind? How has he been a Father in your life?

3. Reflecting on John 17:20–26, have you experienced any gaps between *knowing* that God loves you and *receiving* God's love emotionally or *extending* that same love to others? If so, what makes it difficult for you to let the reality of God's love sink deep into your life and being?

4. Read Hebrews 4:16. Do you approach God's "throne of grace with confidence" when you pray? Why or why not?

5. How does our world see God's love in Christians today? How is that view of God's love obscured at times—and what can we do to change that?

6. How could you become more aware of the Spirit's presence in your daily life and especially in your prayers?

Exercise in Prayer

Praying the Scriptures

There are many ways you can pray the words of Scripture, but try this: *paraphrase* and *place* yourself in the story. The words of the Bible give us an opportunity to direct God's words back to him in the form of prayer. Take a verse or two from your devotional time, a favorite Bible passage, a prayer recorded in the Bible, or perhaps a psalm; then, rephrase the words to compose your own prayer to God.

- Praying Psalm 23 can bring peace to a troubled mind.
- Praying Psalm 100 can inspire sincere praise.
- The optional Bible reading in each session of this study provides a passage that can be turned into your own paraphrased prayer.

Finding yourself in a familiar Bible story can also incite your soul to prayer. Stories from the Gospels about Jesus are particularly helpful for engaging your imagination. Here are five simple steps you can take:

1. Read the story, such as the Prodigal Son (Luke 15:11–32) or the healing of the woman who bled for twelve years (Mark 5:25–34).

2. Place yourself in the story as a bystander observing or as one of the characters.

3. Ask questions to become part of the story: What do I see? Hear? Feel? Smell or taste?

4. What words, themes, or images come to mind as you reflect on this story?

5. How are you now moved to pray and talk with God?

Involving the creative capacities of our imagination in prayer can open up new avenues for spiritual growth and depth in our relationship with the Lord.

Notes

Notes

2 THE FATHER'S KINGDOM

Your Kingdom Come

The Father's Kingdom

Have you ever taken a long road trip? I have wonderful memories of packing up our young children in the car and leaving our cares behind. We set out from Tennessee and headed south to Florida. The kids immediately started asking, "Are we there yet?" … and a few minutes later, "Are we there yet?" At which point I started questioning my life decisions!

We celebrated when we saw the welcome sign into the sunshine state, crossing the border into Florida. Then we counted down miles to Jacksonville … and then Daytona Beach. Soon the road signs began pointing us to Orlando. We began seeing signs advertising the wonders that we would experience when we reached our destination—Disney World, the magic kingdom ruled by a mouse! Every road sign that counted down the miles and every billboard advertising our destination raised our hopes and excitement … and the noise level in the car.

As Jesus-followers, we are on a long journey toward an everlasting kingdom ruled by our everlasting King. We eagerly wait to experience the fullness of the Lord's kingdom in our world: *Is it close? Are we there yet?* The Lord knows that our hearts were made for his kingdom. And as we wait, we pray, "Your kingdom come."

Read It

Key Bible Passage

For this session, read Jesus' parable about the coming kingdom in Luke 19:11–27. Jesus told this story just before he entered Jerusalem riding a donkey and a young colt as the coming King.

Optional Reading

Observe the prophet Isaiah's description of the coming kingdom and the reign of the King in Isaiah 11:1–10.

"Your kingdom come ... "

MATTHEW 6:10

Know It

1. In the first century when the disciples prayed, "your kingdom come," what were likely their expectations about the coming kingdom? What do you envision when you make that same request today?

2. In Jesus' parable, what was the king trying to learn about his servants by entrusting them each with ten minas (three month's wages) while he was away?

3. From the optional reading of Isaiah 11:1–10, what characteristics of the King and his kingdom do you observe?

Explore It

Parable of the Ten Minas

Jesus' story in Luke 19:11–27 about a ruler who traveled to a distant land to receive a crown before returning to his homeland would've been something his first-century listeners could easily relate to from their own recent history.

After having served as governor of Galilee, Herod the Great traveled to Rome around 40 BC to be crowned king of Judea. Herod had to take his kingdom by force and put down a revolt, but the Roman Senate granted him a crown and the authority to rule. In 4 BC, Herod Archelaus, a son of Herod the Great, made the same journey to receive a crown. Archelaus was very unpopular at the time, so rather than making him a king, Rome made him an *ethnarch*, a position with less authority than a king.

The Herods were known as demanding rulers who maintained strict systems of accountability within their domain. Failing to use resources wisely or, even worse, rebelling against their rule would have brought severe penalties. The implications for the accountability to Jesus' authority and his expectations of faithfulness are as clear today as they were when he first told the parable.

> "Sin must be fought, Satan must be resisted, sickness must be prayed over and groaned under (Romans 8:23), and death must be endured until the second coming of the King and the consummation of the kingdom."
>
> —John Piper

Praying for God's Kingdom

It is somewhat startling to hear in the Lord's Prayer King Jesus himself request that the kingdom come. Jesus is God who took on the flesh and bone of humanity to reveal to us what God is like and to bridge the gap between heaven and earth. His kingdom was announced by his presence in our world, and it was inaugurated by his sacrificial death and his victory over death through his resurrection. Jesus sits at God the Father's right hand on the throne of heaven (Heb. 12:2), but we do not yet experience the full benefits of his reign on earth.

Human history is a story of rebellion against the rule of God. In Genesis 3, the first humans rebelled against God and obeyed the orders of a creature rather than the Creator. God established the first man and woman, Adam and Eve, as his image bearers and regents over the plant and animal kingdom. They were to rule and exercise dominion over God's creation, but a serpent who should have been a subject of the man and woman instead exercised dominion over them. Ever since that moment, our earth and all humanity have been caught up in the pain of rebellion against the rightful King.

Reminders that God's kingdom is not yet here are all around us. Just read news headlines and you'll see stories about war and violence, injustice and unrest, animosity between different points of view and people groups, stories of premature death, and the painful effects of natural disasters and diseases. God always rules over all, but we do not yet experience this fully. However, when we pray for God's kingdom to come, God responds to our prayers. In his plan, our lives also become a reminder that his kingdom is coming when we bring the values of his future kingdom into practice today. This is why we pray for the kingdom to come.

Live It

In God's coming kingdom, we will know the righteousness, justice, and peace all people desire. In this life, we don't experience that kingdom in full, but we do find a foretaste of it. As part of the body of Christ on earth, we are called to be a sign and symbol of that coming kingdom. When we experience the bonds of community, when we share in the joy of giving, when the gospel is received and changes a life, when a child is baptized, when we extend ourselves to serve and reach out to someone else in love, when our hearts are united in worship—we are pointing to the reality of the coming kingdom.

The signs are exciting and encouraging, but they're only a small glimpse of the glory and greatness that is to come. Jesus' kingdom is coming, and it is our hope. As we live a life of faithfulness with the gifts and callings God has entrusted us with, we become like road signs telling the world that God's kingdom is ahead; we're almost there.

> "The church lives in the midst of history as a sign, instrument, and foretaste of the reign of God."
>
> — LESSLIE NEWBIGIN

Life Application Questions

1. When you consider Jesus' life and ministry on earth, what were some of the signs that the kingdom of God was breaking into human history?

2. What are some of the gifts, relationships, and opportunities that Jesus has entrusted you with?

3. When you consider your accountability with what Jesus has given you, how do you think he might respond to your stewardship of those gifts?

4. List one thing you know God desires to see happen in the following areas:

- Your marriage and/or family: ______________________
- Your work and/or ministry: ______________________
- Your nation and other nations: ______________________
- Your local church: ______________________

Consider how you can bring the values of the coming kingdom into practice in those areas.

5. What would it look like for your life and your church to be a "road sign" for the kingdom of God?

6. When you reflect on the coming kingdom, what captures your imagination most and gives you hope?

Exercise in Prayer

Three P's of Prayer

Anyone who has tried to focus on developing a robust prayer life has faced the problem of distractions. The three P's of prayer can help you adjust your routine and minimize distractions.

- POSTURE

  Pray sitting, standing, kneeling, lying down, and even while walking, running, or exercising. If you tend to pray in the same position regularly, try a different posture to enter into your time of prayer.

  You can also find unique opportunities to pray. Do you commute to work? Offer up a prayer for God's blessing for the day while sitting on the subway or stuck in traffic. Are you a long distance runner? Pray for specific people in your life as you reach different mile-markers.

- PLACE

  A quiet, secluded spot works best for many people. This may be a corner of a room, a chair on a porch, a quiet table at a coffee shop, or a prayer room at church. Any place can become a place for prayer. Jesus often removed himself from others to spend time in prayer in quiet places (Mark 1:35).

- PRESENCE

  Rather than spending all of your energy on what you might say to God or what you need from him, consider sitting quietly and becoming consciously aware of his loving presence. You could begin by simply saying, "It's me again, Lord." Sing a few lines from a favorite song and then sit quietly and patiently before talking with God. Much of the beauty and value in prayer comes from simply being in God's presence.

We could also add a fourth P for a *passage* of Scripture. Meditating on a Bible passage or verse can clear your mind and focus your conversation with God. Not sure which to choose? Try beginning your prayer time reciting the words of Deuteronomy 6:4–5: "Hear, O Israel; The LORD our God, the LORD is one. Love the LORD your God with all your heart and with all your soul and with all your strength."

Notes

Notes

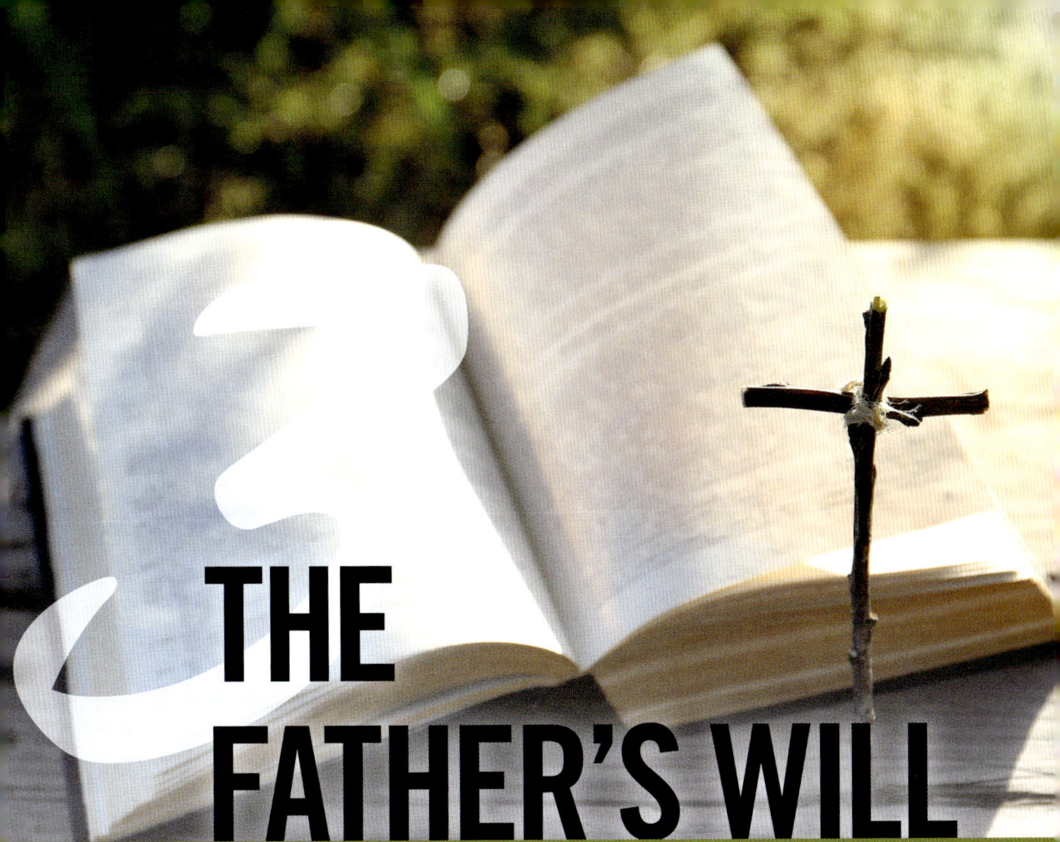

3

THE FATHER'S WILL

Your Will Be Done

The Father's Will

God is sovereign over all his creation, yet not everything that happens in our lives and in our world can be considered God's *will*. Events and tragedies occur that God did not *want, desire,* or *cause* to happen. If, even today, we are still praying as Jesus taught us, "your will be done, on earth as it is in heaven" (Matt. 6:10), then sometimes, something less than God's will must be still occurring in our world.

This prayer request for the Father's will to be done is vitally important because God desires good for us and for the world he has made. Yet our world is still struggling with the painful effects of sin.

God reigns as the sovereign over all the earth and over all history. His ultimate purposes will not be frustrated. He will create good even out of the evil that we experience. As Scripture reminds us, "We know that in all things God works for the good of those who love him, who have been called according to his purpose" (Rom. 8:28). Not everything that happens in our lives will be good, but God will work all things in our lives out for our good and his glory. This is part of our motivation in praying for his will to be accomplished on earth just like it is in heaven.

Read It

Key Bible Passage

For this session, read Jesus' prayer in the garden of Gethsemane as he struggled with the Father's will in Matthew 26:36–46.

Optional Reading

From Romans 8:18–39, observe how we struggle with the effects of sin and wait with hope for God's will to be done on earth as it is in heaven.

"Your will be done, on earth as it is in heaven."

MATTHEW 6:10

Know It

1. What are some things you observe in Matthew 26:36–46 about the relationship between Jesus and God the Father?

2. How might our world be different if God's will that is accomplished in heaven were completed in the same way on earth?

3. From the optional reading, what hope do you find in Romans 8:18–39, although we live on an earth where God's will is not yet accomplished like it is in heaven?

Explore It

The Prayer of Indifference

In the year 1491, Inigo Loyola was born into a family of Basque nobility in modern-day Spain. He grew up with a desire to serve as a knight, winning fame, fortune, and glory. When he was eighteen years old, he began serving a Spanish Duke. He quickly rose through the ranks to attain the position of "servant of the court" due to his diplomatic leadership and military skills.

St. Ignatius of Loyola

Just before turning thirty, Loyola's life direction changed when a cannonball ricocheted off a wall, smashing his right leg. He endured multiple surgeries where his bones were set and rebroken (all without anesthetics) and was left with a significant limp, because his right leg remained shorter than the left. During his recovery, he began reading the Bible and other Christian literature. He not only was moved to put his faith in Jesus, but also to devote the rest of his life to serving the Lord.

Using a variation on his first name, *Ignatius,* he studied theology and eventually began a religious order. He taught others the spiritual practices he used while recovering from his wounds, and he published a guide, *Spiritual Exercises,* to help others use the same practices.

Among the prayer practices Ignatius taught is the prayer of indifference. When his life direction was abruptly changed, he had to find a way to discern God's path for his life and to give his heart room to grow in a new direction. The prayer of indifference was part of that process. This kind of prayer has been described by author Ruth Haley Barton like this:

> In the context of spiritual discernment, indifference is a positive term signifying that "I am indifferent to anything but God's will." This is interior freedom or a state of openness to God in which we are free from undue attachment to any particular outcome. ... We ask God to bring us to a place where we want "God's will, nothing more, nothing less, nothing else."

This is a specific way to offer the kind of prayer our Lord raised up to God the Father in the garden of Gethsemane: "Father ... not as I will, but as you will" (Matt. 26:42).

> "The basic purpose of prayer is not to bend God's will to mine, but to mold my will into his."
>
> —Timothy Keller

Live It

The scene recorded in Matthew 26 of Jesus in the garden is one of the most emotionally raw accounts in the whole Bible. Jesus—knowing that his betrayer was on the move with armed soldiers to arrest him and fully realizing the humiliating and painful death awaiting him—opened his heart up to the Father and surrendered his will to our greatest good.

The garden of Gethsemane today is a beautiful, peaceful spot, situated on the hillside of the Mount of Olives just east of Jerusalem. Because of the garden's elevation overlooking Jerusalem, the city gates and pathways leading up the mountain are clearly visible.

Mount of Olives, Jerusalem

In this spot, Jesus would have easily been aware that a troop of soldiers coming to arrest him were making their way out of the city and up the paths leading to the garden. With just a few more steps up to the top of the Mount of Olives, Jesus could have walked down the other side and disappeared into the Judean wilderness. He wasn't caught by surprise by the traitor Judas and the armed soldiers. He stayed in the garden praying because he loved us and was willingly to lay down his life so that we could receive new and everlasting life.

We may not face a literal crucifixion or a midnight struggle of prayer in Gethsemane, but we all are called to sacrificially love others with the same type of love we have received from Jesus. Loving people like that means making our own midnight prayers from time to time and discovering what it looks like to surrender our will and desires over to God's direction.

Life Application Questions

1. What are some painful results in our world or in your own life experience of God's will not being fully completed right now on earth?

2. How do you distinguish between what God *wants* to happen and what he *wills* to happen? Why is that distinction important?

3. What are some practical strategies or tools you can use to discern God's direction and will for your life?

4. Part of God's will being done on earth is his will being done *in* and *through* believers (for example, 1 Thess. 4:3; 5:18; 1 Peter 2:15). What are some examples of God working in and through the church today to accomplish his will?

5. Is something preventing you from offering up a "prayer of indifference" to God? How could you grow toward making that type of prayer?

6. Write out your own prayer of indifference, expressing your desire for nothing more and nothing less than the will of God for your life and for those you love. Consider making this prayer part of your regular prayer time.

Exercise in Prayer

Journaling as Prayer

Consider how journaling could become part of your prayer routine, not only as a replay of your prayers but as part of your intentional reflection on your conversations with God. Many of us have probably used prayer lists to organize our thoughts and requests, but a journal would take that practice another step forward by examining our internal thoughts, feelings, and changes in prayer.

- One type of journaling could include a record of prayers made and prayers answered. This can be a faith-building exercise that allows you to look back over the ways God demonstrates his faithfulness over time.

- You may also want to try writing a letter to God. Writing requires greater specificity of thought than speaking. Penning a letter to God could be a way for you to clearly identify your struggles and lay them before the Lord, to express gratitude for God's faithfulness, and to worship the Lord for specific qualities that inspire your praise.

- Journaling could also help you explore your emotional responses in prayer and identify particular words, images, or themes. How has prayer changed your perspective? How has your appreciation of the character and person of God grown through prayer?

Notes

4 OUR DAILY BREAD

Give Us Today

Our Daily Bread

Day by day and with each passing moment,
Strength I find to meet my trials here.

Trusting in my Father's wise bestowment,
I've no cause for worry or for fear.

He whose heart is kind beyond all measure,
Gives unto each day what he deems best—

Lovingly, its part of pain and pleasure,
Mingling toil with peace and rest.

—Lina Sandell, "Day by Day" 1865

These are lines from one of the 650 songs written by Lina Sandell. Lina was Swedish, lived during the nineteenth century, and saw the beginning of the twentieth before her passing. Her deep expressions of faith were used in Christian revivals throughout Sweden before being translated into English.

Lina learned the truth of God's daily care and provision for his children even in seasons of intense heartbreak. When she was in her twenties, she was crossing a lake with her father when her father drowned in a boating accident before her very eyes. Several years later, while processing her grief, she penned the words that have brought comfort and reassurance in the hymn, "Day by Day."

This song captures the heart of dependence that motivates us to ask God to provide just what we need, "our daily bread."

Read It

Key Bible Passage

For this session, read Jesus' teaching about dependence on God's care from Matthew 6:25–34 and Matthew 7:7–11.

Optional Reading

Remember the help that is available from Jesus when we approach him in prayer from Hebrews 4:14–16.

"Give us today our daily bread."

MATTHEW 6:11

Know It

1. In Matthew 6:25–34, what reason does Jesus give for why we have no cause for worry or anxiety?

2. Jesus chose to use "birds of the air" and "flowers of the field" to teach about the Father's love. What simple things do you notice in your world that remind you of God's care?

3. From the optional reading, how is Jesus prepared and capable to be attentive to our prayers and needs (Hebrews 4:14–16)?

Explore It

Bread for Each Day

The word translated *daily* in the request for our daily bread is a Greek word that is so rare some scholars have suggested that it was created by Christians. The word is *epiousion* and it appears only in the Lord's Prayer in Matthew's and Luke's gospels.

Because there are few other ancient sources where the word is used, it is difficult to translate *epiousion* into English. Possible translations include "for the coming day," "necessary," "for today," or "for tomorrow." Considering the options, "daily" is a faithful translation. It conveys the idea that we continually live with a spirit of dependence on the goodness of God to provide what we need each moment.

Daily bread in the Lord's Prayer echoes words from the Old Testament book of Proverbs:

> Give me neither poverty nor riches,
> but give me only my daily bread.
> Otherwise, I may have too much and
> disown you and say, 'Who is the LORD?'
> Or I may become poor and steal,
> and so dishonor the name of my God.
>
> PROVERBS 30:8–9

Bread in both the Lord's Prayer and in this short prayer from Proverbs implies sustenance. It's about our heavenly Father gifting us with enough of what we need to get us through each day. Trusting God daily for our "bread" means we are not expecting extravagance, but we are boldly expecting God to care for us on an as-needed basis. When God meets our daily needs, we live a life of constant, faithful dependence on the gracious hand of our God to satisfy not our indulgent wishes, but our essential needs.

Sitting on a hillside overlooking the Sea of Galilee, Jesus directed people to look at the birds in the air and the wildflowers flourishing in the fields before reminding them that God would surely take care of them:

> *"Look at the birds of the air; they do not sow or reap or store away in barns, and yet your heavenly Father feeds them. ... See how the flowers of the field grow. They do not labor or spin. ... If that is how God clothes the grass of the field ... will he not much more clothe you?" (Matt. 6:26, 28–30)*

It is because we have a Father in heaven who loves us that we can trust in Jesus' words: "But seek first [God's] kingdom and his righteousness, and all these things will be given to you as well" (Matt. 6:33).

Meditation on a Hazelnut

"All shall be well, and all shall be well, and all manner of thing shall be well."

What is your immediate reaction to these words? Do you find this notion reassuring, or do you tend to instinctively push back against it because it sounds like something from a greeting card?

In reality, this statement has far greater depth than a simplistic slogan. These words come from the pen of Julian of Norwich, written more than six hundred years ago. Her book, *Revelations of Divine Love,* is believed to be the oldest book in English written by a female author.

Although life was very different in her time compared with our modern world, Julian's experience bears some striking similarities to ours today.

- When she was a young girl living in or near the second greatest city in England at the time, Norwich, the bubonic plague rolled through and claimed the lives of one-third to one-half of the local population. Periodically, throughout her life, this plague would spring back up with devastating results.
- When she was about thirty years old, she nearly died. She faced an unknown illness, and her family prepared for her death.
- At some point after her near-death experience and as a single woman, Julian chose the life of an anchoress for a church in Norwich. Becoming an anchoress meant living a secluded life dedicated to prayer. She lived in solitude, interacting and communicating with the outside world from her window, never leaving her room. (If you've lived

through the days of COVID-19 and remained "safer at home" or experienced quarantine, then maybe you can identify with her just a little bit.)

Julian recorded a series of revelations, one of which included considerations of a small hazelnut. The hazelnut, to her, seemed so small and insignificant that it might vanish away into nothingness—until she made three observations from the hazelnut: *God made it. God loves it. God keeps it.*

Sometimes our life seems so small and insignificant that we're on the verge of vanishing away into nothing. However, the truth is that God made you, God loves you, and God will keep you—through pandemics and illness, through isolation and loneliness, through healing and victory, through celebration on the other side of the challenges you are facing right now.

Proclaiming "All shall be well, and all shall be well, and all manner of thing shall be well" is not a greeting card or a carefree song. It's a radical declaration of faith in the God who made us, loves us, keeps us, and gives us our daily bread.

If you've been struck by worry, fear, or trouble, take heart and listen to the last verse of the hymn "Day by Day."

Help me then, in every tribulation,
So to trust Thy promises, O Lord,

That I lose not faith's sweet consolation
Offered me within Thy holy Word.

Help me, Lord, when toil and trouble meeting,
E'er to take, as from a father's hand,

One by one, the days, the moments fleeting.
'Till I reach the promised land.

Life Application Questions

1. If our heavenly Father knows our needs, why do you think he wants us to ask him for our daily bread?

2. What are your daily needs? Do you distinguish them from your daily *wants*? If so, how?

3. Do you depend on Jesus or do you look to your own resources to satisfy your desires and meet your needs? How could you depend on Jesus more intentionally?

4. When in particular has the Lord demonstrated his faithfulness to you by meeting your needs?

5. Instead of pursuing satisfaction of all of our desires, what does Jesus instruct us to do in Matthew 6:33? How might we practically follow his instructions?

6. What do you worry about? Write out and offer up a prayer of dependence on God to meet the needs that cause you to worry.

Fasting and Prayer

In Matthew's gospel, the Lord's Prayer in chapter 6 is part of Jesus' Sermon on the Mount. Chapter 6 opens with Jesus reminding his listeners not to practice their acts of righteousness for the purpose of being seen by others (Matt. 6:1). Then, he explains what that means for three core religious practices of first-century Judaism:

- Giving (verses 2–4)
- Praying (verses 5–15)
- Fasting (verses 16–18)

Let's focus on the third one, fasting. This is a time-tested spiritual practice that sharpens our awareness of our dependence on God and our need for him. In our world of abundance, fasting has a way of reminding us that everything we enjoy—food, strength and health, resources—is a gift from God.

Jesus cautioned us that fasting is not something we do to receive a reward or to be noticed by others, but that fasting presents its own secret reward: "When you fast, put oil on your head and wash your face, so that it will not be obvious to others that you are fasting, but only to your Father, who is unseen; and your Father, who sees what is done in secret, will reward you" (Matt. 6:17).

One way to begin fasting is by eliminating a daily meal and using that mealtime instead for prayer and reflection. Some people also give the money they would've spent on the meal to a charity that helps people in need. You might also choose to fast for a longer time period, such as twelve or twenty-four hours. (Be aware of medical limitations and consult a doctor before fasting if you have any medical concerns.)

The practice of fasting often accompanies an important decision point or seeking God's help in a particularly difficult situation. However, we can also incorporate fasting into our regular spiritual routines. As we experience feelings of physical hunger, our spiritual senses are often sharpened. Fasting from food helps us direct our attention on the Lord and our energy on pursuing our relationship with him.

Notes

Forgive Us Our Debts

Our Debts

A survey of Jesus' teachings in the Gospels will quickly reveal a common thread—or a bottom line—that comes down to loving God and loving others (see Matt. 22:37–40). We can express this love in many different ways, but forgiveness is a real test of the sincerity of our love. God proves his love for us by offering us forgiveness for our sins, or in the words of the Lord's Prayer, our *debts* or *trespasses*. We demonstrate our love for others by forgiving them.

If we are not moving toward forgiveness, then we are demonstrating our limited grasp of the gracious, unmerited, and abundant way that God has offered us forgiveness in Christ. If we hold onto every slight, nurture every wound, and cultivate a revengeful, bitter attitude—then it's almost impossible for us to come before God and claim the forgiveness that he offers us. People who won't admit they've been wrong and need forgiveness have a very difficult time forgiving anyone else.

In the Lord's Prayer, we ask for God's forgiveness of our wrongs and remind ourselves to forgive others the same way God has forgiven us—*freely.*

Read It

Key Bible Passage

For this session, read Jesus' teaching about the fig tree that concludes with instructions about forgiveness in Mark 11:12–25.

Optional Reading

Observe King David's experience of confession and forgiveness recorded in Psalm 32.

"And forgive us our debts, as we also have forgiven our debtors."

MATTHEW 6:12

Know It

1. Put yourself in the story of Mark 11. Imagine anticipating a nourishing snack of fresh fruit only to be disappointed upon closer inspection of the tree. What do you see and hear as Jesus curses the fig tree and then later clears the temple court? How would you feel? How might you respond?

2. Why do you think Jesus connected his teaching on forgiveness with the object lesson of the fig tree?

3. From the optional reading, what are some of the blessings connected with forgiveness in Psalm 32?

Explore It

Mark 11 begins with Jesus entering Jerusalem, riding on a donkey and a colt on Sunday of the week that he knew he would be crucified. The people waved palm branches and shouted words of praise. Jesus continued going up into the temple grounds, and he looked around carefully and then went back home (Mark 11:11). He was visiting Jerusalem for the Passover feast and likely staying with his friends Lazarus, Martha, and Mary just outside Jerusalem in the village of Bethany.

As he and his disciples returned to Jerusalem the next morning, Jesus was hungry. He saw a fig tree full of leaves. It was early spring. Ripe figs wouldn't be available until late spring or early summer. But, when the tree is full of leaves, it should also be producing buds or green figs that are good for eating. This tree, although full of leaves, had no green buds, which meant it would produce no fruit that year. Jesus cursed the tree. This is the only time we have a record of Jesus using his power destructively.

Debts vs. Trespasses

The New Testament uses several Greek words to describe sin. The Lord's Prayer in the gospel of Matthew uses the word *ophelema* which is rendered *debt* (Matt. 6:12). However, only two verses later, the gospel uses *paraptoma*, which is usually translated as *trespass* (Matt. 6:14). In all cases, sin is what separates us from God, our friends, and our family. Without forgiveness—whether it be forgiving *debts* or *trespasses*—relationships suffer and redemption is not possible.

Jesus continued his walk to the temple courts, specifically an outer court, the Court of the Gentiles. This court was the nearest a non-Jewish person could get to the temple. It was supposed to be set aside for prayer and worship, but instead it had been turned into a place of business. People who traveled from distant places would exchange their money for the shekel in order to pay the temple tax, while others would purchase animals for sacrifice. Jesus stopped that practice for at least a day to restore the area to a place of prayer and worship for gentiles. He overturned the tables of moneychangers and drove out merchants.

The next morning, the disciples noticed the cursed fig tree had withered, and Jesus followed up with a challenging teaching:

> *When you stand praying, if you hold anything against anyone, forgive them, so that your Father in heaven may forgive you your sins. (Mark 11:25)*

Mark sandwiches Jesus' clearing of the temple courts between the account of the fig tree being cursed and then withering. The gospel writer is carefully crafting a warning for the first communities of Christians who received his gospel—and also for us.

The Accursed Fig Tree by James Tissot

Jesus carefully inspected the center of Israel's worship at the temple. But instead of finding a place of prayer, he found a place of greed; instead of a house of worship, he found a house of commercial enterprise. From a distance, the temple was bustling with religious activity and it appeared to be healthy, vibrant, and full of life. But upon closer inspection, there was no faithfulness, no dependent trust in God. It was like a fig tree full of leaves, but no fruit.

We would be wise to pay attention to this warning as well and to avoid an appearance of faith without substance. We may be able to recite the words in the Lord's Prayer without hesitation, but an authentic faith and understanding of God's mercy toward us is revealed by our willingness to freely forgive those who trespass against us.

The Two Parts of Forgiveness

Forgiveness involves acknowledgment and release.

- Before forgiving, we acknowledge that a wrong was done. Some of us trip over this first step toward forgiveness because we have a hard time saying, "I'm wounded. You hurt me. In fact, I still hurt." This acknowledgment requires vulnerability that overcomes our pride.

- After acknowledging our wound, we have the opportunity to release someone else from the penalty box in our soul. We give up our need to punish them. We let go of our ability to manipulate them or make them pay. Sometimes we give up our right to demonstrate their guilt and our innocence, to tell the world, "They were wrong, and I was right." That's not easy. That's sincere love.

It's important to note that forgiving doesn't mean that reconciliation with the other person will (or should) happen or that every broken relationship will heal, but it does mean that you open a pathway for the healing of your own soul. Forgiving means you are progressing in a life of authentic faith in a superficial world.

Live It

In Mark 11, the disciples knew that the fig tree died by Jesus' words rather than natural causes because it withered from the root up. A tree that had become parched or temporarily lacked sufficient water would wilt from the leaf to the branch. But this tree was dead from the root to branch to leaf!

As our faith grows deeper, we become better equipped to forgive others. It's important to remember that when Jesus instructs us to pray, "Forgive us our debts, as we also have forgiven our debtors," he is not teaching that we must earn God's forgiveness by forgiving others; this is not a quid-pro-quo arrangement. When we forgive, we are not making a deposit in a forgiveness account that we can one day withdraw when we need divine forgiveness. As we put our roots down deep into God's love for us, we are better able to express our love for others through forgiveness. It is the fruit of a life of deep and strong faith. If we care for the unseen parts of our life, the visible parts of our life will remain healthy. In other words, care for your root and the fruit will take care of itself.

> "We forgive with no strings attached; that may require us to forgive repeatedly. When we do, we shock the world with God's power at work within us."
>
> —Rebecca Nichols Alonzo

Life Application Questions

1. What is the relationship between receiving forgiveness from God and offering forgiveness to others?

2. Can you remember a time when you felt truly and fully forgiven? How would you describe that experience?

3. How do you distinguish between reconciliation and forgiveness? Is it possible to forgive someone but not reconcile with him or her?

4. What role does confession play in forgiveness—yours, another person's, and corporate confession?

5. What can make forgiveness so difficult? And how can we overcome those obstacles?

6. Is there someone you need to forgive or ask to forgive you? What is one next step (big or small) that you can take toward forgiveness?

Exercise in Prayer

Praying ACTS

The acronym ACTS is a time-tested structure that many believers have used to infuse new life into their prayer time.

ADORATION

Praise God for who he is. You can select different character qualities or attributes to focus your thoughts and begin your prayer by worshiping the Lord. This practice retrains your thoughts and adjusts your mental perspective to step into conversation with God.

CONFESSION

Identify and admit your shortcomings to the Lord. He already knows us thoroughly, but confessing our faults develops a spirit of humility, raises awareness of our struggle with sin, and helps facilitate a vital experience of forgiveness.

THANKSGIVING

Express gratitude for what God has done. Observe and verbalize the ways that you've experienced God's goodness. This cultivates a grateful spirit that continues outside your prayer time.

SUPPLICATION

Bring your requests to God. We don't command God, but we are encouraged to clearly and boldly ask for his help. This helps us grow in our conscious dependence on God and will help us become more aware of how he is working in our lives and world.

Notes

Notes

6 OUR TEMPTATIONS

Deliver Us from the Evil One

Our Temptations

Do you remember that feeling when you approached final exams in school? There was that intense sense of pressure building. Yet there was also an assurance that your instructors were not aiming to cause you to fail but doing whatever they could to help you pass the test.

Life brings us to points of testing, moments that we aren't certain we can move beyond, unsure whether we'll pass the test. Life's tests aren't presented as examinations in a classroom. They sneak up on us and take different forms: the loss of a loved one, a chronic illness, a severe financial strain, or a broken relationship.

These moments of testing can quickly become opportunities for temptation to strike. As pastor and author Darrell Johnson observes, "There are events or experiences in life through which the Father intends to prove and improve our character and faith, but the evil one sneaks in and intends to destroy our character and faith." Times of testing will come to all of us, and temptation from the evil one is usually not far behind. No wonder the Lord's Prayer concludes with a petition for deliverance from that which leads us astray from our heavenly Father.

Read It

Key Bible Passage

For this session, read how Jesus faced and overcame temptation in Matthew 4:1–11.

Optional Reading

Observe the prayer requests the apostle Paul sent to the church at Thessalonica in 2 Thessalonians 3:1–5.

"And lead us not into temptation, but deliver us from the evil one."

MATTHEW 6:13

Know It

1. What strategies did Jesus use to withstand temptation in the wilderness in Matthew 4:1–11?

2. God specifically allowed Satan to tempt (or test) Jesus in the wilderness (Matt. 4:1). What purpose in the life and ministry of Jesus might this have served?

3. From the optional reading, how does directing our hearts into "God's love and Christ's perseverance" (1 Thess. 3:5) protect us from the evil one?

Explore It

Temptations and Tests

Two strong nouns dominate the final petition in the Lord's Prayer. Most English translations us the word *temptation* at the end of the first clause and *evil* or *the evil one* to finish the second clause: "Lead us not into temptation but deliver us from the evil one." These words in Greek are *peirasmos* (temptation) and *poneros* (evil or evil one). *Peirasmos* can refer to temptation toward sin or evil, but it can also refer to a testing or time of trial. It's used in Greek literature to describe the process of refining gold, where gold is mined from rock and then undergoes *peirasmos*—a refining to bring the precious metal out of the rock and also to demonstrate that it really is gold.

We know that God does not tempt us with evil (James 1:13). He never pulls us toward sin. However, God does allow situations to occur that test our faith and character and motivate us to grow stronger in the face of adversity. It is in these moments of challenge that our enemy invades to offer a temptation that could make us fall:

> *Be alert and of sober mind. Your enemy the devil prowls around like a roaring lion looking for someone to devour. (1 Peter 5:8)*

This is why we plead with the Lord to lead us away from temptation and protect us from the traps of the evil one. When those times of testing, trial, and refining come, we must stand firm on the promises of God's Word:

> *God is faithful; he will not let you be tempted beyond what you can bear. But when you are tempted, he will also provide a way out so that you can endure it. (1 Cor. 10:13)*

The Devil's Tactics

Our enemy, the devil, uses the same tactics that have worked for centuries to draw people toward sin. Be on guard by watching out for these five signs of temptation:

1. **Sowing Suspicion**

   When Satan approached Eve in the garden of Eden, he began by asking, "Did God really say, 'You must not eat from any tree in the garden'?" (Gen. 3:1). Our enemy tries to make us suspicious of God's care and concern, of his provision, of his power, and of his goodness. If our faith begins to waver, it's easier for us to fall to temptation.

2. **Encouraging Entitlement**

   In 2 Samuel 11, King David seemed to feel that the normal rules that governed human behavior (even divine commandments) no longer applied to him. He saw a beautiful woman (Bathsheba), sent messengers to retrieve her, and he slept with her with no regard for her, her husband, the marriage covenant, or for the consequences of his action. When we begin to think that we are entitled to special treatment and perks and that rules don't apply to us, we are in danger of falling into sin—with damaging consequences to us and those around us.

3. **Spreading Blame**

   In Genesis 3:12, after God confronted Adam with his sinful disobedience, Adam responded, "The woman you put here with me—she gave me some fruit from the tree, and I ate it." Adam tried blaming Eve, as well as God, rather than acknowledging his own actions. If we fail to accept responsibility for ourselves, we can become a prey for the enemy's snares.

4. **Feeding Fear**

Jesus, I will stick with you to the end. These other guys, I'm not sure about, but you can count on me! That's basically what Peter promised the Lord in John 13. But after Jesus was arrested in the garden of Gethsemane, Peter ran. Later, Peter denied three times that he even knew who Jesus was (John 18). When fear begins to cloud our minds, our decision-making becomes unsteady and can lead us into a trap.

5. **Magnifying the Negative**

Satan used this tactic (as well as others) when tempting Jesus in the wilderness: *Look out there, Jesus, just stones, hot, dry, dirty, dusty rocks. No trees, no water, no grass, just rocks. You haven't eaten for forty days. If you are the Son of God, turn the stones to bread!* Satan was using Jesus' relationship with God the Father as a dagger to twist: *If you are God's Son, why are you in this situation? If God loves you, why would he allow this?* By focusing on the negative and jumping to conclusions from difficult circumstances, we fall into Satan's trap.

"Submit yourselves, then, to God. Resist the devil, and he will flee from you."

JAMES 4:7

The Doxology

Some churches recite the Lord's prayer with a final line, called a doxology: "*For yours is the kingdom and the power and the glory forever. Amen.*" This is also found in some Bible translations as the end of verse 13 in Matthew 6.

The oldest and most trustworthy New Testament manuscripts do not contain this ending of the Lord's Prayer. It's most likely that the original prayer given by our Lord did not contain this particular phrase either, but that it was added later by Christians who made the Lord's Prayer part of their spiritual life. It may have even been a congregational response when the prayer was offered up publicly by a church leader.

It's hard to imagine why the earliest New Testament scribes would have deleted this part of the prayer from their biblical text if it had been in the Lord's Prayer originally. However, it's easier to understand why it may have been added. This kind of ending to prayer was common in Jewish and early Christian tradition.

Jesus' model prayer for his disciples bears some similarity to an ancient prayer used in Jewish worship called the *Kaddish.* Here is part of the text of that prayer:

> *Exalted and hallowed be God's great name, in the world which God created, according to plan. May God's majesty be revealed in the days of our lifetime and the life of all Israel—speedily, imminently. To which we say: Amen.*

Both the Lord's Prayer and the Kaddish are rooted in the Hebrew Scriptures. As David prepared his son Solomon and God's people for the work of building the temple, he offered the following prayer of dedication and worship. (Notice the similarity to the doxology of the Lord's Prayer.)

> *Yours, Lord, is the greatness and the power and the glory and the majesty and the splendor, for everything in heaven and*

earth is yours. Yours, Lord, is the kingdom; you are exalted as head over all. (1 Chronicles 29:11)

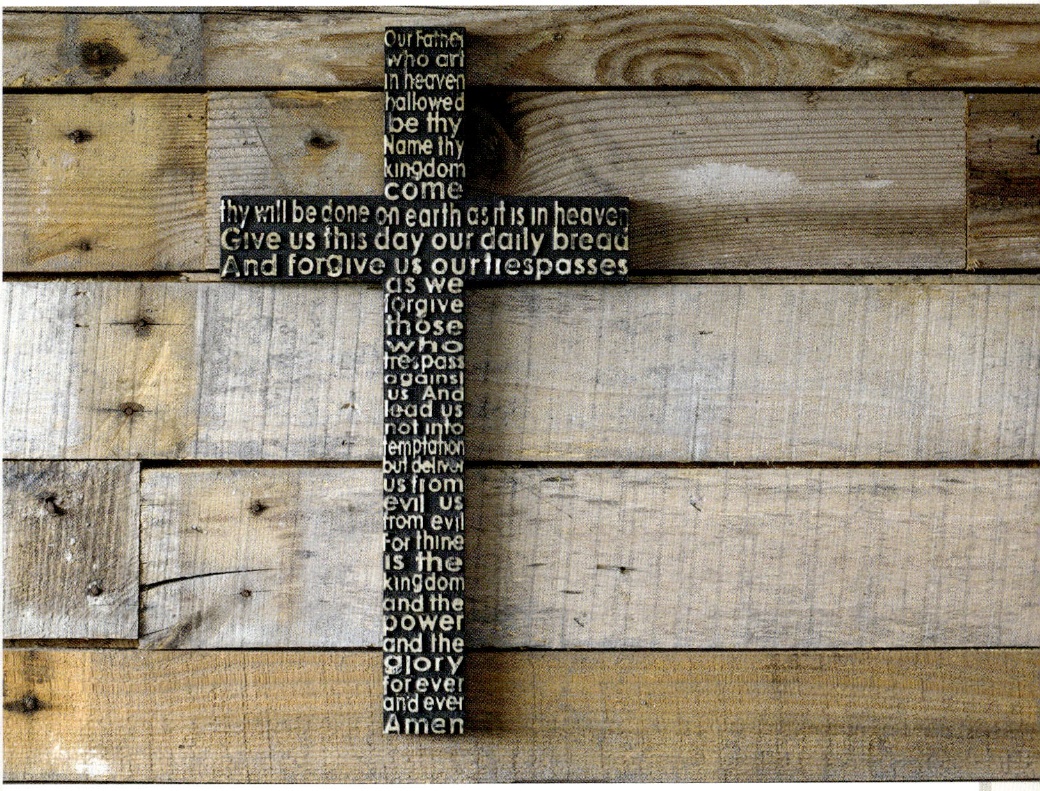

Live It

If you've ever had the experience of losing electricity unexpectedly on a dark night, you know how startling and confusing it can be. You've probably fumbled around for matches to light candles or stubbed your toe while looking for a flashlight. You wonder what caused the power outage and if everyone in your house is safe.

Moments of testing can feel like the lights have gone dark in our soul. We can't see things clearly. We're startled and unsure. We worry about ourselves and our loved ones. In those moments, we can become vulnerable to Satan's traps. We might walk right into them because we are confused, groping through the darkness.

We need to find a light in order to avoid the traps. Our heavenly Father is the one who provides the light that overpowers the darkness of evil—the evil that tries to turn our moments of testing into temptation, the evil that lurks in our path to trap us, the evil that we seem to carry around with us. As the psalmist declares to the Lord, "Your word is a lamp for my feet and a light on my path" (Ps. 119:105).

"I am the light of the world. Whoever follows me will never walk in darkness, but will have the light of life."

JOHN 8:12

Life Application Questions

1. What are some examples in which moments of testing can easily turn into opportunities for temptation?

2. When have you experienced a season of testing or trial? Were you also challenged by temptation during that time?

3. Are you aware of potential vulnerabilities to temptation that you are guarding against? If so, what are some guards that help you fend off the devil's attacks?

4. How did Jesus' security in his relationship with God the Father help him overcome temptation?

5. What can you do to build up your confidence in the Lord's unfailing love for you as a safeguard against temptation?

6. Write your own personalized version of the Lord's Prayer, making it relevant to what you're facing in your life now.

	THE LORD'S PRAYER	YOUR PERSONALIZED PRAYER
	Our Father in heaven	
1	Hallowed be your name	
2	Your kingdom come	
3	Your will be done on earth as it is in heaven	
4	Give us today our daily bread	
5	And forgive us our debts as we also have forgiven our debtors.	
6	And lead us not into temptation	
7	But deliver us from the evil one	

Practicing the Presence of Jesus

Brother Lawrence was a seventeenth-century Carmelite monk who became known for his life of devotion to the Lord and his joy in the simple tasks of life. He joyfully lived a life of prayer as he worked in the kitchens and later as a cobbler in a monastery. In his classic book, *The Practice of the Presence of God,* he wrote:

> I cannot imagine how religious persons can live satisfied without the practice of the presence of God. For my part I keep myself retired with Him in the depth and center of my soul as much as I can. While I am so with Him I fear nothing; but the least turning from Him is insupportable.

Practicing the presence of Jesus in our lives means becoming aware that the Spirit of Christ is with us at all times. We are never alone. Every part of our day is filled with new joys when we realize that Jesus is participating with us.

Here are three ways to intentionally raise your awareness of Jesus' presence in your life.

- **Create routines of prayer.**

  Schedule regular times of prayer throughout the day. These don't have to be lengthy sessions but can be brief and focused, although regular. You could even set reminders on your phone and use a timer to stay on track.

- **Visit with other people.**

  Take time to see other people, not as appointments in your calendar, problems to solve, or sales calls to make, but as individuals who bear the image of God. Look past the surface to see their humanity, and you will find the reflected image of the Creator in them.

- **Slow down.**

  In our fast-paced world, our minds become harried by constant demands for attention and muddled with a range of complex thoughts and emotions. Create a sustainable pace of life that allows you to process the events of your day, your week, your month, and then present the details of those events to the Lord.

Notes

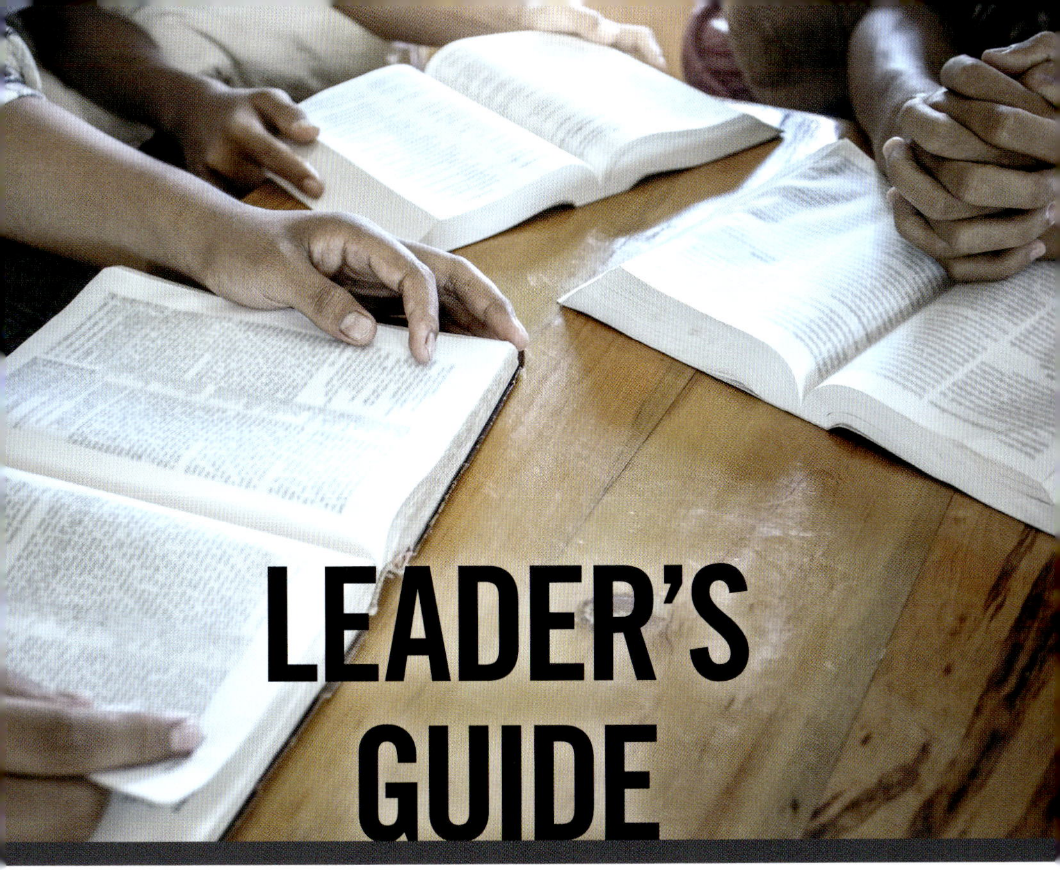

LEADER'S GUIDE

"Encourage one another and build each other up."

1 THESSALONIANS 5:11

Leader's Guide

Congratulations! You've either decided to lead a Bible study, or you're thinking hard about it. Guess what? God does big things through small groups. When his people gather together, open his Word, and invite his Spirit to work, their lives are changed!

Do you feel intimidated yet?

Be comforted by this: even the great apostle Paul felt "in over his head" at times. When he went to Corinth to help people grasp God's truth, he admitted he was overwhelmed: "I came to you in weakness with great fear and trembling" (1 Corinthians 2:3). Later he wondered, "Who is adequate for such a task as this?" (2 Corinthians 2:16 NLT).

Feelings of inadequacy are normal; every leader has them. What's more, they're actually healthy. They keep us dependent on the Lord. It is in our times of greatest weakness that God works most powerfully. The Lord assured Paul, "My grace is sufficient for you, for my power is made perfect in weakness" (2 Corinthians 12:9).

The Goal

What is the goal of a Bible study group? Listen as the apostle Paul speaks to Christians:

- "Oh, my dear children! I feel as if I'm going through labor pains for you again, and they will continue until *Christ is fully developed in your lives*" (Galatians 4:19 NLT, emphasis added).
- "For God knew his people in advance, and he chose them *to become like his Son*" (Romans 8:29 NLT, emphasis added).

Do you see it? God's ultimate goal for us is that we would become like Jesus Christ. This means a Bible study is not about filling our heads with more information. Rather, it is about undergoing transformation. We study and apply God's truth so that it will reshape our hearts and minds, and so that over time, we will become more and more like Jesus.

Paul said, "The purpose of my instruction is that all believers would be filled with love that comes from a pure heart, a clear conscience, and genuine faith" (1 Timothy 1:5 NLT).

This isn't about trying to "master the Bible." No, we're praying that God's Word will master us, and through humble submission to its authority, we'll be changed from the inside out.

Your Role

Many group leaders experience frustration because they confuse their role with God's role. Here's the truth: God alone knows our deep hang-ups and hurts. Only he can save a soul, heal a heart, fix a life. It is God who rescues people from depression, addictions, bitterness, guilt, and shame. We Bible study leaders need to realize that *we can't do any of those things*.

So what can we do? More than we think!

- We can pray.
- We can trust God to work powerfully.
- We can obey the Spirit's promptings.
- We can prepare for group gatherings.
- We can keep showing up faithfully.

With group members:

- We can invite, remind, encourage, and love.
- We can ask good questions and then listen attentively.
- We can gently speak tough truths.
- We can celebrate with those who are happy and weep with those who are sad.
- We can call and text and let them know we've got their back.

But we can never do the things that only the Almighty can do.

- We can't play the Holy Spirit in another person's life.
- We can't be in charge of outcomes.
- We can't force God to work according to our timetables.

And one more important reminder: besides God's role and our role, group members also have a key role to play in this process. If they don't show up, prepare, or open their hearts to God's transforming truth, no life change will take place. We're not called to manipulate or shame, pressure or arm twist. We're not to blame if members don't make progress—and we don't get the credit when they do. We're mere instruments in the hands of God.

"I planted the seed, [another] watered it, but God has been making it grow. So neither the one who plants nor the one who waters is anything, but only God, who makes things grow."

1 CORINTHIANS 3:6–7

Leader Myths and Truths

Many people assume that a Bible study leader should:

- Be a Bible scholar.
- Be a dynamic communicator.
- Have a big, fancy house to meet in.
- Have it all together—no doubts, bad habits, or struggles.

These are myths—even outright lies of the enemy!

Here's the truth:

- God is looking for humble Bible students, not scholars.
- You're not signing up to give lectures, you're agreeing to facilitate discussions.
- You don't need a palace, just a place where you can have uninterrupted discussions. (Perhaps one of your group members will agree to host your study.)
- Nobody has it all together. We are all in process. We are all seeking to work out "our salvation with fear and trembling" (Philippians 2:12).

As long as your desire is that Jesus be Lord of your life, God will use you!

Some Bad Reasons to Lead a Group

- You want to wow others with your biblical knowledge.

  "Love . . . does not boast, it is not proud" (1 Corinthians 13:4).

- You're seeking a hidden personal gain or profit.

  "We do not peddle the word of God for profit" (2 Corinthians 2:17).

- You want to tell people how wrong they are.

  "Do not condemn" (Romans 2:1).

- You want to fix or rescue people.

  "It is God who works in you to will and to act" (Philippians 2:13).

- You're being pressured to do it.

  "Am I now trying to win the approval of human beings, or of God?" (Galatians 1:10).

A Few Do's

✔ Pray for your group.

Are you praying for your group members regularly? It is the most important thing a leader can do for his or her group.

✔ Ask for help.

If you're new at leading, spend time with an experienced group leader and pick his or her brain.

✔ Encourage members to prepare.

Challenge participants to read the Bible passages and the material in their study guides, and to answer and reflect on the study questions during the week prior to meeting.

✔ Discuss the group guidelines.

Go over important guidelines with your group at the first session, and again as needed if new members join the group in later sessions. See the *Group Guidelines* at the end of this leader's guide.

✔ Share the load.

Don't be a one-person show. Ask for volunteers. Let group members host the meeting, arrange for snacks, plan socials, lead group prayer times, and so forth. The old saying is true: Participants become boosters; spectators become critics.

✔ Be flexible.

If a group member shows up in crisis, it is okay to stop and take time to surround the hurting brother or sister with love. Provide a safe place for sharing. Listen and pray for his or her needs.

✔ Be kind.

Remember, there's a story—often a heart-breaking one—behind every face. This doesn't *excuse* bad or disruptive behavior on the part of group members, but it might *explain* it.

A Few Don'ts

✘ Don't "wing it."

Although these sessions are designed to require minimum preparation, read each one ahead of time. Highlight the questions you feel are especially important for your group to spend time on.

✘ Don't feel ashamed to say, "I don't know."

Disciple means "learner," not "know-it-all."

✘ Don't feel the need to "dump the truck."

You don't have to say everything you know. There is always next week. A little silence during group discussion time, that's fine. Let members wrestle with questions.

✘ Don't put members on the spot.

Invite others to share and pray, but don't pressure them. Give everyone an opportunity to participate. People will open up on their own time as they learn to trust the group.

✘ Don't go down "rabbit trails."

Be careful not to let one person dominate the time or for the discussion to go down the gossip road. At the same time, don't short-circuit those occasions when the Holy Spirit is working in your group members' lives and therefore they *need* to share a lot.

✘ Don't feel pressure to cover every question.

Better to have a robust discussion of four questions than a superficial conversation of ten.

✘ Don't go long.

Encourage good discussion, but don't be afraid to "rope 'em back in" when needed. Start and end on time. If you do this from the beginning, you'll avoid the tendency of group members to arrive later and later as the season goes on.

How to Use This Study Guide

Many group members have busy lives—dealing with long work hours, childcare, and a host of other obligations. These sessions are designed to be as simple and straightforward as possible to fit into a busy schedule. Nevertheless, encourage group members to set aside some time during the week (even if it's only a little) to pray, read the key Bible passage, and respond to questions in this study guide. This will make the group discussion and experience much more rewarding for everyone.

Each session contains four parts.

Read It

The *Key Bible Passage* is the portion of Scripture everyone should read during the week before the group meeting. The group can read it together at the beginning of the session as well.

The *Optional Reading* is for those who want to dig deeper and read lengthier Bible passages on their own during the week.

Know It

This section encourages participants to reflect on the Bible passage they've just read. Here, the goal is to interact with the biblical text and grasp what it says. (We'll get into practical application later.)

Explore It

Here group members can find background information with charts and visuals to help them understand the Bible passage and the topic more deeply. They'll move beyond the text itself and see how it connects to other parts of Scripture and the historical and cultural context.

Live It

Finally, participants will examine how God's Word connects to their lives. There are application questions for group discussion or personal reflection, practical ideas to apply what they've learned from God's Word, and a closing thought and/or prayer. (Remember, you don't have to cover all the questions or everything in this section during group time. Focus on what's most important for your group.)

Celebrate!

Here's an idea: Have a plan for celebrating your time together after the last session of this Bible study. Do something special after your gathering time, or plan a separate celebration for another time and place. Maybe someone in your group has the gift of hospitality—let them use their gifting and organize the celebration.

	30-MINUTE SESSION	60-MINUTE SESSION
READ IT	Open in prayer and read the *Key Bible Passage.* 5 minutes	Open in prayer and read the *Key Bible Passage.* 5 minutes
KNOW IT	Ask: "What stood out to you from this Bible passage?" 5 minutes	Ask: "What stood out to you from this Bible passage?" 5 minutes
EXPLORE IT	Encourage group members to read this section on their own, but don't spend group time on it. Move on to the life application questions.	Ask: "What did you find new or helpful in the *Explore It* section? What do you still have questions about?" 10 minutes
LIVE IT	Members voluntarily share their answers to 3 or 4 of the life application questions. 15 minutes	Members voluntarily share their answers to the life application questions. 25 minutes
PRAYER & CLOSING	Conclude with a brief prayer. 5 minutes	Share prayer requests and praise reports. Encourage the group to pray for each other in the coming week. Conclude with a brief prayer. 15 minutes

90-MINUTE SESSION

Open in prayer and read the *Key Bible Passage.*

5 minutes

- Ask: "What stood out to you from this Bible passage?"
- Then go over the *Know It* questions as a group.

10 minutes

- Ask: "What did you find new or helpful in the *Explore It* section? What do you still have questions about?"
- Here, the leader can add information found while preparing for the session.
- If there are questions or a worksheet in this section, go over those as a group.

20 minutes

- Members voluntarily share their answers to the life application questions.
- Wrap up this time with a closing thought or suggestions for how to put into practice in the coming week what was just learned from God's Word.

30 minutes

- Share prayer requests and praise reports.
- Members voluntarily pray during group time about the requests and praises shared.
- Encourage the group to pray for each other in the coming week.

25 minutes

Group Guidelines

This group is about discovering God's truth, supporting each other, and finding growth in our new life in Christ. To reach these goals, a group needs a few simple guidelines that everyone should follow for the group to stay healthy and for trust to develop.

1. **Everyone agrees to make group time a priority.**
   We understand that there are work, health, and family issues that come up. So if there is an emergency or schedule conflict that cannot be avoided, be sure to let someone know that you can't make it that week. This may seem like a small thing, but it makes a big difference to your other group members.

2. **What is said in the group stays in the group.**
   Accept it now: we are going to share some personal things. Therefore, the group must be a safe and confidential place to share.

3. **Don't be judgmental, even if you strongly disagree.**
   Listen first, and contribute your perspective only as needed. Remember, you don't fully know someone else's story. Take this advice from James: "Be quick to listen, slow to speak, and slow to become angry" (James 1:19).

4. **Be patient with one another.**
   We are all in process, and some of us are hurting and struggling more than others. Don't expect bad habits or attitudes to disappear overnight.

5. **Everyone participates.**
   It may take time to learn how to share, but as you develop a trust toward the other group members, take the chance.

If you struggle in any of these areas, ask God's help for growth, and ask the group to help hold you accountable. Remember, you're all growing together.

Notes

Notes

Quote Sources

Lesslie Newbigin, *The Open Secret* (Eerdmans, 1995).

John Piper, "Is the Kingdom Present or Future?" (Desiring God Foundation, February 4, 1990).

Ruth Haley Barton, *Pursuing God's Will Together: A Discernment Practice for Leadership Groups* (IVP Books, 2012).

Timothy Keller, *The Encounters with Jesus Series VIII: The Obedient Master* (Dutton, 2013).

Carolina Sandell, "Day by Day" translated by A. L. Skoog (1865).

Rebecca Nichols Alonzo, *The Devil in Pew Number Seven* (Tyndale Momentum, 2010).

Darrell Johnson, *Fifty-Seven Words that Change the World* (Canadian Church Leaders Network, 2005).

Brother Lawrence, *The Practice of the Presence of God: The Best Rule for a Holy Life* (Christian Classics Ethereal Library).